CW00429876

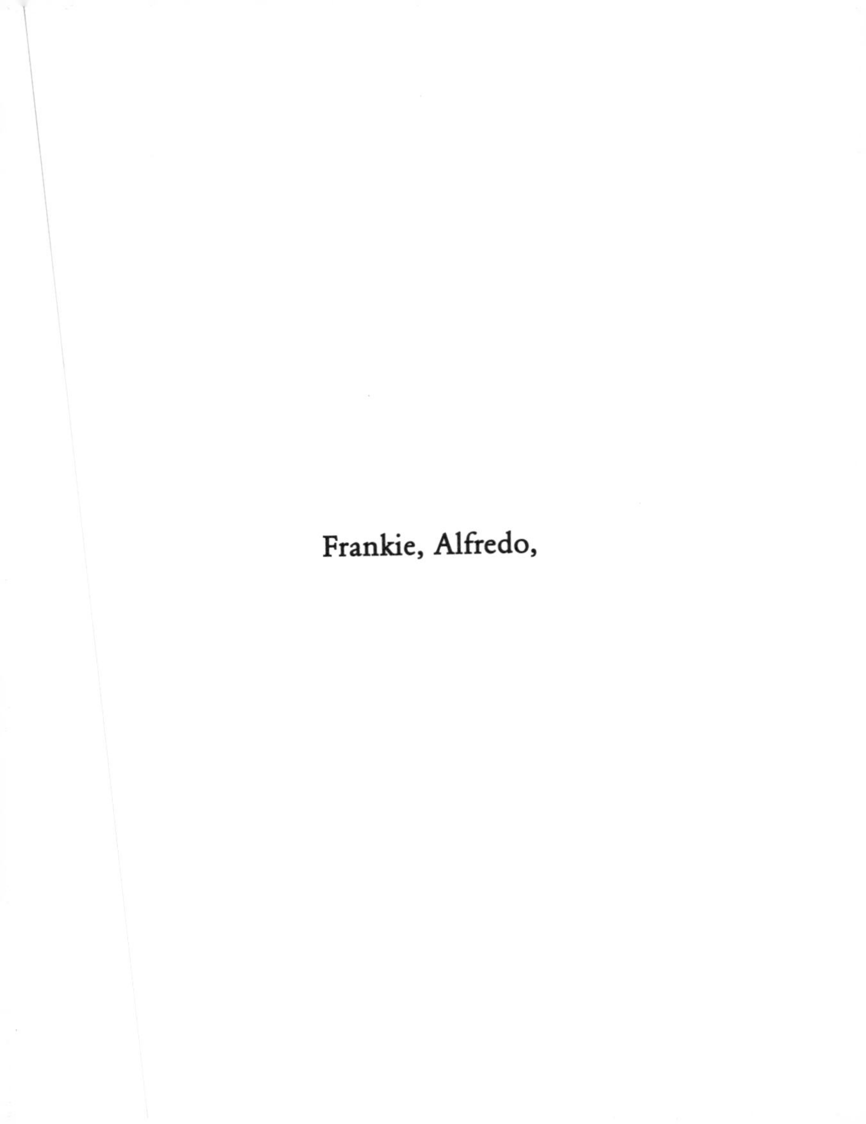

Frankie, Alfredo,

Liane Strauss was born in Queens, New York, and lives in London. She teaches creative writing and literature at Birbeck College, University of London, and at City Lit. Her first full collection, *Leaving Eden*, is forthcoming from Salt Publishing.

For Margaret –
with very best wishes
[illegible]
May 2009

Frankie, Alfredo,

Liane Strauss

Donut Press

Published by Donut Press in April 2009.

Donut Press, PO Box 45093,
London, N4 1UZ.
www.donutpress.co.uk

Printed and bound by
The Colourhouse,
Arklow Road Trading Estate, Arklow Road,
London, SE14 6EB.

Donut Press gratefully acknowledges
the support of Arts Council England.

ISBN: 9780955360459

Copyright © Liane Strauss, 2009.
All Rights Reserved.

The right of Liane Strauss to be identified
as author of this work has been asserted
in accordance with Section 77 of the
Copyright, Designs and Patents Act 1988.

A CIP record for this book is available
from the British Library.

LOTTERY FUNDED

In memory of Berthe Restatcher Machbitz

Acknowledgements

Acknowledgements are due to the editors of the following publications and websites where some of these poems first appeared: *Ask for It by Name* (Unfold Press, 2008), *Future Welcome: The Moosehead Anthology X* (DC Books, 2005), *The Hudson Review*, *The Like of It* (Baring & Rogerson, 2005), *Limelight* (www.thepoem.co.uk), *nthposition* (www.nthposition.com), *Poetry Daily* (www.poem.com), *Prairie Schooner*, *Rising*.

'Childhood', previously titled 'Two Worlds', received a Commendation in the National Poetry Competition 2002.

Contents

Alone in the Night

after Li Ch'ing Chao

Emergency rescue has just freed
the woman trapped for twelve hours
underneath the ice. As I drink
a peach schnapps my hypothermia rises
in a fine vapour from my heart, streams
round the lonely peach stone of my cheek.
The room is unsteady, as if it were drunk.
I try to write a poem in which
two ice floes drift and dissolve like willows.
My cold cream has gone off.
My hairclip's yanked too tight.
I throw myself into my black bathrobe,
collapse back onto the gold couch and crush
the phoenixes in your Peterson's Guide.
A lone, deep ice cube chinks
like the last nickel lost in Atlantic City.
In the bitter loneliness of the window
I search for just one small watery
streak of day. Without even an old movie,
I lie changing channels in a blue light.

Boy

Years before, the infant Salome had a favourite
she called Boy. He was always there, wrist-first,
heel-first, a lassoed cowboy dragged through
girlhood's surface-of-the-moon terrain,
kissing the cliff-face of her bed, his mouth around her hair.
And knowing he was hers,
belonged exclusively to her, she loved him.

Love was not enough or she would never have lost
Boy, naked, nameless, stupid and alone, under a Waldbaums sky
coffered in coffee-stained acoustic tile and hyperlit
like human skin under the microscope of teenage lust,
below the shadow of the precipice down which,
split and paired and glistening exactly like the sometime necks
of smallish animals or great big birds,
pomegranates, like molten rivers, ran.

Back home she turned merciless. She snapped
the head off every last doll she possessed
and heaped the headless bodies on her bed.
She wept longer than anyone ever wept
and every night she dreamed of Boy,
only of him, his moulded-plastic head
mouldering in the dust of crates and cabbage leaves.

This, to satisfy those for whom cause and explanation,
and not the simple disposition of parts, is paramount.

Ditchdigger

If one's years can't be better employed than
in sweating poesy, a man had better be a ditcher. – Lord Byron

I have a friend who has a friend whose father dug ditches,
which my friend had to admit he never had.
"A hole, sure, deep and wide enough to accommodate
a substantial root system, transplant
a good-size yard-shrub maybe. But a ditch, that's
something different. A ditch takes hours,
takes a man into the ground up to his shoulders.
You don't get strong from ditchdigging,
and you don't get healthy, but like my friend
likes to say, 'One thing's certain
when you get up every morning to dig a ditch:
you know where you are. My father'd always say,
"The day I stop digging ditches'll be the day
they find me in one I was very nearly done with." ' "

Rumour

I'm not making this up.
I heard of a girl once who caught it
clear across a banquet hall
just from listening to
the confections of some confabulator.

Well, he was quite a talker
and, like the champagne,
the more he poured the more she frothed
until she was so intoxicated by the feeling
that she had to tell somebody
that she wanted to tell everybody.

She needn't have worried.
Like an airbourne influenza, word got around.
The more it talked, the more it grew,
until at last and finally
it overwhelmed her. That's how it is.
In vino veritas, of love she flew.

Such things occur, I know, because
it was talk you took me with –
strange talk, and beautiful, and full of pity.
As I recall (I don't recall, I'm elaborating)
you went straight to my knees
one hundred proof, straight bourbon, bang
straight to my head like backwoods bootleg.

Ever since, everything out of my mouth
is pure you. Your words keep
flaring up in me like fever, the stamp
of your expression on my tongue
like fog-bound battalion phantoms on an inkpad.
And oh, my *imprimatur*, to overhear you talk me,
like a gosling unsteadily imprinting –
it was nearly my undoing!

Suddenly I'm aware that everyone everywhere
is talking us, *mon amour*.
We've become the rumour of each other.
And that rumour's growing, picking up momentum
like a meteor coming for me.
Already in the swelling shadow
of its all-consuming darkness
I'm disappearing like a mid-century politician,
because what's love but a Molotov cocktail
of what has and hasn't and has yet to happen
and ten thousand times as strong as anything you never tell me.

Poetry Lover

after Catullus X

"I was innocently perambulating the poetry section
when your *cavaliere* fell upon me like a sword."
Varus had been telling me about him ever since we'd met,
and while they bandied the ins and outs of an indecorous word
which one of them had lately come upon, his eyes
roaming my *Campus Martius*, his mouth
wrestling the smile that sputtered and flickered
like a dodgy filament into submission,
I inferred the wattage of his intelligence.
And it was then I noticed his hands,
which were rather small, and clever,
like a couple of Marx brothers,
and which even seemed to be pacing,
black cuffs flapping behind them like coattails,
and how much I liked the seemingly uncalculated mix
of reticence and daring
when he sidled in between myself and Varus.
We exchanged some *à propos*
that quickly transposed into repartee –
the poetry scene in the States
where he had just been promulgating
his most recent prize-winning collection,
how well it was selling, how handsomely
they'd paid him for his university readings,
especially at Harvard;
his American hosts, how well-off they were
and the preposterous show they'd made

of merely subsisting on their intellectual shoestrings,
eschewing red meat and pumping iron
almost as remorselessly as they pumped him
for particulars of Life in England;
putting him up at the home of the chair
of the English department.
You stayed with Harry Levin?
Our eyes locked, his glittering with a pleasure
I had come perilously close to wanting to learn the inside of.
I didn't expose him for a fraud and an impostor
(Harry Levin being dead these eighteen years),
but it wasn't long before I broke it off with Varus
and swore off the whole perfidious breed,
since male poets can't seem to tell the difference
between lies of art
and the delicate exigencies required when speaking with a lady.

Hymn

before a bust of Sappho

Immortal Aphrodite, though in your eyes
neither mercy nor the hunger of desire
can be detected, since they lie in your head
like the impress of a leaf in snow,
at full tilt you are riding here now,
the wings of your sparrows in my ears beating,
my heart demented and refusing to heed me.
I can see you will not be deterred.

So I implore you, Dread Goddess,
since you turn your cold ear to my tormented lips,
inspire me to your likeness in marble
that no one can see through me
and never, never in a thousand years guess
at the conversations that keep running with him in my head.

Three Ostriches

1

I know that from out there
there seems a lot to envy.
Legs long as summer afternoons
and quick as convertibles.
Feathers creamy and light
as French puff pastry.
But where there's stature
there isn't always depth.
Everything I know I've learned
from keeping an eye on the world
at the end of my periscope neck.
I lay gorgeous, enormous eggs
and hatch the most beautiful babies.

2

Oh! There are birds that can fly!
Birds with songs, that can sing!
Birds who, white on water, glide
while I can only walk or run
as primitive as a man.
On the day I realized,
like a felled tree I collapsed,
my poor knees buckled back,
thump, in a great roar of dust
like some defenestrated sack
for everything I know I lack.
On the next I hung my shingle,
Plumes for hats, for hire, for quills.

3

I know that from out there
with my feathers in the air
and my neck like a third leg
and my head like a spade
I might look a bit risible.
But don't buy the bad press.
It's not that I'm afraid.
I'm not hiding my head;
I'm giving it a rest,
getting it out of the heat,
letting my great bulk have a think.
I find treasures all the time.
And it's so wonderful to be invisible.

Childhood

Somewhere there are twelve children playing in a field.
Somewhere there are twelve children playing on a road.
Each of the children has a name and is nameless.
Each of them has a mother and father and is orphaned.
Each has seen the sky and bitten through a blade of grass –
yellow or green as the rain proposed.
Each has saved a beetle from murderous hands
and murdered a beetle with a small placid crack.
Each has flown the flight of the fly, with its buzz,
and a fighter plane, and a buzzard.
Each has said one thing and thought another.
Each has said one thing and meant another.
Each has said nothing and thought nothing and been nothing.
Each has thought, "I am a cloud. I am thunder. I am a beetle,"
running down the field, or the road, chasing a ball.
Each has made a world disappear,
seen another rise up out of oceans to meet it.
Each has seen one piece of grass become a field.
Each has gone from standing in the wood
to pinching one leaf on a road.
We are always falling through the road onto the field
or out of the field onto the road.
Twelve children chase a ball.
There are twenty-four children.
The children chase the ball,
half red, half yellow, now blue, now green,
that gets away from them and rolls.

The Museum of Desires

Here are the thoughts you can't have
And here are the feelings you can't touch,
Melting like pictures you can't save
From burning buildings while you watch.

These are the loves you can't tell,
Locked in the quarry like ice in your veins,
Like beautiful lines you didn't spell
And beautiful scenes on a dark stage.

The hut from a past you can't name,
An exquisite shroud embroidered with rot,
An infant skull, the horn of a ram,
The relic's sacred martyred heart.

Here is an echo you can't hear.
Here is a cup and here are the kisses
Counted and numbered and bound and hidden
In secret vaults and shatter-proof cases.

The Seamless Future

In the future, sidewalks won't have cracks,
not on purpose or from bad planning.
There'll be no thresholds: doors
will open out of walls like in old houses
with fascinating secrets, but without hinges.
No one will hesitate, wondering whether to go in.
No one will slip on grout or catch a heel
in gaps of cobble mortar – all the stumbles
will dissolve and fade from conversation.
Windows will obscure like walls, walls
clarify like butter, undetected.
In imitation of the ease with which dawn slips past
the most fanatic lookout every morning,
the made world will come to echo the given
until finally, in a perfect marriage of the natural
and the artificial, the world will be seamless.

And then our inner lives, as if they were chameleons
and envious of the outer ones, will also even,
and love won't come in patches
but like whole cloth off the bolt,
mixed feelings blending like acrylics,
wisdom running ribbon
without frays or hitches, belief, desire,
inseparable from proof and gratification,
thought and action and reflection
no longer discrete acts of theatre, but like waters,

lapping, overlap until they deliquesce together.
Being in all ways as we seem to ourselves, seeming
to others just as we are, we too will be seamless.

Given time, even you and I will emulsify,
not remember where we end
or our beginnings, a continent at last, land
into water imperceptibly slipping, sea into ether.
The horizon won't have any.
There'll be nowhere to lay anchor.
Face and fathom, like hours,
like every disappearance, seamless.

Transcriptions of Éluard

On the day of the eclipse, when time collapsed
midnight into noon and we stopped, along
with every moving thing and every growing thing
upon the living surface of the shadowed planet,
we proved beyond the shadow of a doubt
we still believed in something like a God
enough to still believe what turned its back
staked all our love against indifference.
And all day under the spell I remembered
the eager boy that summer in Avignon
delivering transcriptions of Éluard on blue paper,
how carefully he began to dress, and your long hair,
and how I used to navigate the corridor as if I always wore
a careless coy chignon in hot weather and take no notice.

Variations on a Theme by Lady Suwō

Pillowed on your arm
only for the dream of a spring night,
I have become the subject of gossip,
although nothing happened.

Pillowed on your dream,
I come and go all spring,
taking pleasure in gossip
as though nothing happened.

Pillowed on my arm,
I confide only in myself
the dream of your arm,
my endless dream of your arm.

Pillowed on my dream,
I no longer drift out into a spring night
but make plans before sunset,
as if something happened.

Pilloried by love
I sip the dram of gods
from the spring of night –
Where's the harm in that?

Pillowed on the dream of your arm,
a mute owl on a bare bough
in a starless barn
shrouded in snow.

Disarmed by a spring night,
powerless against dreams,
assailed by gossip,
I throw the windows open.

Pillowed on the spring night
of your arm –
I can't sleep!

Pillowed on the gossip of your arm
I have become an object of ridicule
in my own eyes.

Pillowed on your *nothing*,
only for the dream of a spring *nothing*,
I have become the subject of *nothing*,
although *nothing*.

Pillowed on *his* arm
all night, all spring,
that the gossip may reach even to your dreams.

In my dream I am pillowed on your arm
and the clouds of a spring day
keep changing faster than gossip
or an emu running backwards.

Although nothing happened,
nothing happened
that hasn't already happened again.

Also noting happenstance.
Alto notes sing half steps.
Altered knots have ends.
All through knowing happiness.

Like the subject of gossip
as it begins to spread,
I keep your pillow
between my legs.

If nothing happened,
why has my pillow become
harder than your arm?

You
and your pillow
and your arm
and your dream
and your spring night
and your gossip.
As if.

L'oreiller de ton nez
que pour une belle nuit d'été
je suis devenue sujet
de ce rien qui n'est passé.

A Pillow, a Dream and an Arm
walk into a bar …

It wasn't your arm.
It wasn't spring.
It wasn't night.
It wasn't a dream.
It isn't gossip.
Nothing never happens.

Night, spring, dream
of gossip
for on
the arm
a Pillowed
happened
your only I
become
the have nothing subject of
although …

Although nothing happened,
I have become the subject of gossip,
only for the dream of a spring night
pillowed on your arm.

Archimedes and Me

It's the morning after the deluge
and I'm walking down Northern Boulevard
just past the LensCrafters (or is it a Pearle Vision?)
when I have this great idea for a movie.
It opens on you and me, Archie,
or two people just like you and me,
walking down Northern Boulevard – and I,
the way they say Balzac composed, pacing,
start speaking one part, then the other,
back and forth, back and forth –
and the one who's like me turns
to the one who's like you and says,
"I have this great idea for a movie,"
and the one who's like you turns
to the one who's like me and says, "Yes?"
in that mock-indulgent tone you adopt
whenever you don't want me to know
how adorable you find me, and the one
who's like me says, "Yes," as if she
hasn't noticed that he's looking at her
like a proof-reader scanning the final proofs
for that something that has so far
eluded his notice. "It's about us,
or two people just like us, and one of them
comes up with a great idea for a movie
and the other one makes like he's sceptical,
but he isn't, really; really, he's every bit

as keen as she is." And as the one who's
playing me is telling the one who's playing
you, *he* gets that sceptical look on *his* face
that, when you get it, really means you're
remembering something we were doing
last night, or imagining something
we may be doing later, but the one who's me
just forges ahead, laying it all out until she's done.
Then she turns to the one who's you and says,
"So what do you think?" And he turns
to her and says, "That sounds like a great idea."
And she says, "Really? Do you really think so?"
And he says, "Yes. I really think so.
It sounds like a very good idea indeed."
And she says, "Are you sure? Are you really sure?
You don't seem sure." And that's when I step
in a puddle the size of a bathtub
so that I have to take a step backwards
to avoid getting both feet wet,
and that's when I remember, just as when
I really am talking to you, I'm talking to myself again.

Frankie, Alfredo,

after Catullus XVI

I'll give you some of your sour grapes to suck on,
since you suspect my poems only sell because
I tart them up like high school girls in Camden.
A real poet must live in stripy jumpers
and two pair of glasses, eschew irony
and mascara, and tend countrified passions,
lest helpless young men divagate or query
their maudlin eds and over-the-hill tutors,
whose backs are stiff and abacuses rusty
(hence their tendency to curse their barstools, beat
hendecasyllables with lifeless digits,
why they have to pickle their rhetorical
figures in the formaldehyde of bitters).
And you, full of voluptuous objection,
because my verses spill over with push-up
bras and low-riding tangas think I'm a girl!
Name the dawn. I'll take your mouths and your money
both hands tied behind my back, in a blindfold
and ten bona fide inches of stiletto,
one after the other, or both concurrent,
and no seconds. We'll just see who's left standing.

Self-Portrait as Myself

Oh, I've done Socrates and Jesus Christ
off the cuff and, not above a touch of theatre,
Lady Macbeth, with a nod to Ellen Terry.
I confess to smoke and mirrors, stand-ins
like those palindromic Annas, Emmas,
Pips, and Ottos, innocent and flawed
but somehow so convincing
even I have fallen for them.
I've pulled off my beard,
tossed my hat onto the table
and put up that sign that reads:
NO SIGNS
appending the unequivocal rider:
NO PIPES NO PAULS NO PIGMENT
NO SEMAPHORES ALLOWED NO
SUBTLE OR UNSUBTLE GESTURES
NO FANCY PARED DOWN BACK-FORMED
GRECO-LATIN NOMENCLATURE
to become The Allegory of Myself –
a naked canvas, blood-smeared, nerve-
strung, gut-impastoed – stepped back
to see, for myself, if it was true,
and it was honest as the morning,
it beggared blunt, and so revealing
that it thundered like the cavalry with feeling,
fraught to flooding, full to death of meaning.
But it wasn't me.

And since you've come for me
I offer you myself instead,
today, in the image of my dead grandmother –
among my better efforts.
She's in one of her beloved caffs,
Vienna, between the wars,
a back room, gilt and mirrors,
a proscenium of smoke, a fox
dangling from a chair-back
like a provocative suggestion.
Dark and small, in classic
clingy Vionnet, back and shoulders bare,
in quarter profile, turning,
already laughing, already
demurring, her rosewood
scrolls of hair that could have been carved by Gibbons,
a woman of absolutely no convictions
but one or two political connections
(eventually they save her),
who never reserves judgment,
who loves cards
(in fact she is a gifted player),
but whose real genius is for flirting.
She does it all the time, with everyone.
She does it here, in my self-portrait.
Come close, you might catch her even now
regarding her reflection like a man.

The morning is the hardest. It is morning

The morning is the hardest. It is morning
when I nearly don't remember. But I remember
once you said morning should come later,
which never made much sense, until this morning.

The middle of the day, my heart, reminds me
of a road I've never been on, it is endless.
The evening is the hardest, it's the darkness.
I count and hide my eyes until it finds me.

The hours fly off one by one, they leave without me.
I can't keep them and I can't see where they take you.

The night won't end and when you don't forsake me,
stroking my cheek, saying, "You can't come with me,"
it makes no sense, but then the sky is turning
and dark descending dawn dawns and it's morning.

Also available from Donut Press

Stranded in Sub-Atomica, by Tim Turnbull.
£10

Boys' Night Out in the Afternoon, by Tim Wells.
£10

Approaches To How They Behave, by W.S. Graham.
£5

The Adventures of Monsieur Robinet, by John Hegley.
£5

The Observations of Alexandr Svetlov, by Colette Bryce.
£5

Super Try Again, by Roddy Lumsden.
£5

A Voids Officer Achieves the Tree Pose, by Annie Freud.
£5

The Glutton's Daughter, by Sinéad Wilson.
£5

What was that?, by Tim Turnbull.
£5

Buffalo Bills, by John Stammers.
£5

www.donutpress.co.uk